DATE			
2 8			
JAN 1 2			
T2b			

WEASELS, OTTERS, SKUNKS
and Their Family

WEASELS, OTTERS, SKUNKS
and Their Family

by DOROTHY HINSHAW PATENT

Illustrations by Matthew Kalmenoff

Holiday House . New York

I wish to thank Dr. Phillip Wright for the time, interest, and useful information he gave me while I was working on this book.

Text copyright © 1973 by Dorothy Hinshaw Patent
Illustrations copyright © 1973 by Holiday House, Inc.
All rights reserved
Printed in the United States of America

LIBRARY OF CONGRESS CATALOGING IN PUBLICATION DATA
Patent, Dorothy Hinshaw.
    Weasels, otters, skunks, and their family.

    SUMMARY: Introduces the characteristics and habits of various members of the weasel family including the sea and river otter, mink, skunk, badger, and others.
    Bibliography: p.
    1. Mustelidae—Juvenile literature. [1. Weasels]
I. Kalmenoff, Matthew, illus. II. Title.
QL737.C25P29   599'.74447   73–76801
ISBN 0–8234–0228–2

Dedicated to my husband, whose encouragement, suggestions, and practical help made this book fun to write.

CONTENTS

WEASELS, OTTERS, SKUNKS
and Their Family

1 A HIGHLY VARIED FAMILY

Have you ever seen a weasel or a mink, perhaps in a zoo? If you have, you might find it hard to believe that these slim animals are close relatives of the round, fluffy skunk and the fat, lumbering badger. But they are. These animals, and many others, are all members of the weasel family. The scientific name for this family is "Mustelidae." This may seem like a difficult name, but it simply means "weasel family" in Latin. From now on we can call the animals in this family "mustelids" instead of "members of the weasel family."

Most of these fascinating animals have a long body and short legs. Their ears are rounded and usually quite small. All of them produce a strong-smelling liquid called musk. The very unpleasant odor of the skunk comes from an especially potent musk which it uses for defense. Because of their body shape and the shortness of their legs, mustelids have a characteristic bounding run, their backs humping up as they bring their hind legs forward. They often sit up on their haunches with their backs very straight and their ears pricked up, sniffing the air and looking about to spot prey and possible dangers.

Generally the males are bigger than the females; a possible explanation for this, in some cases at least, is discussed later.

Mustelids look for shelter in underground dens, as do many other animals. Some tend to use one den as a home for a long period of time (for example, the Old World badger), while others, such as the mink, use a variety of homes in their wanderings. Some dig their own dens, while others use those made by other creatures, often ones they have eaten.

The Mustelidae are just one family in a larger group of related animals, the order Carnivora—meaning "meat-eaters." Although all the Carnivora eat some meat, many of them eat a variety of foods. Other groups of carnivores are the cat family (Felidae), dog family (Canidae), bear family (Ursidae), and raccoon family (Procyonidae).

The order Carnivora is one division of a still larger group of animals, the class Mammalia. Mammals are animals usually with hair, and they feed their young with milk produced in the mother's body. With two exceptions, they give birth to living young rather than lay eggs. Other mammals include kangaroos, deer, bats, horses, monkeys, whales, and elephants.

The way scientists classify animals shows how closely related they are. Millions and millions of years ago, the different kinds of animals we know today did not exist. They developed very, very slowly, over thousands and thousands of generations. Each generation of animals is very slightly different from the last one. These differences come about in two ways.

Changing Through the Eons

The first way is by the passing on of traits from parents to offspring. Every animal inherits from its parents traits such as the thickness of its fur or the length of its claws, as well as some features of its behavior. Each aspect of every part of us is largely

FISHER

MINK

LONG-TAILED
WEASEL

SHORT-TAILED
WEASEL

MARTEN

LEAST WEASEL

BLACK-FOOTED FERRET

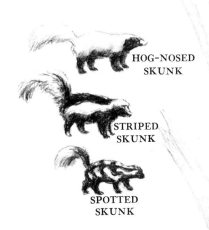

SIBERIAN SABLE

EUROPEAN POLECAT

HOG-NOSED
SKUNK

STRIPED
SKUNK

WOLVERINE

SPOTTED
SKUNK

HONEY BADGER

RIVER OTTER

AMERICAN BADGER

STINK BADGER

SEA OTTER

EUROPEAN
BADGER

The weasel family

inherited. For example, not only is the color of our skin inherited, but also its thickness, oiliness, freckles, and the amount of hair on it. If you think about it for a moment, you will see that there are hundreds of thousands of these traits determining eye color, shape of ears, height, bone structure, and so on.

The information about the traits an animal inherits from its parents is contained in a special chemical code in the egg cell from the mother and the sperm cell from the father. The part of this code which controls one trait is called a gene. When the egg and sperm cells unite, a new combination of genes results, half of them from the mother and half from the father. Each offspring of two parents will inherit a different combination of traits and thus be different from its brothers and sisters. This is one way in which each generation differs from the last one.

There is another cause of differences between generations as well. Sometimes an abrupt change will occur in the chemical code which causes a new trait to appear, one which neither the father nor the mother had. These changes are called mutations. They occur in only about one out of every million egg and sperm cells. Usually they are unfavorable and may cause the animal to die before birth or live but a short life. But occasionally they are favorable and give the animal an advantage of some kind over other animals of its own special kind, or species. Then the animal with the useful mutation has a good chance of surviving to pass on its advantage to its young.

To show how new combinations of traits and mutation could have contributed to the development of different kinds of animals, let us look back millions of years. We will pretend that in a litter of young from some prehistoric mammal there was one animal which inherited a gene for long claws from its father and one for strong claws from its mother. And let's say that another animal in the litter had a mutation which made its muscles work quickly so that it could run faster. Finally, we will imagine a third offspring which did not inherit an especially favorable set of genes and did not have any new traits caused by mutations.

If the animal with the long, strong claws used them for digging, he could dig food out of the ground better and therefore have a good chance of surviving to reproduce. He could also use his improved claws to defend himself more effectively against his enemies. Some of his offspring could inherit his better claws, and they, too, would have a better chance of survival.

The fast animal would also have a good chance of growing up, since he could easily escape from enemies and catch slower-running prey. The animal with no special traits would have less chance of surviving than his better endowed brothers or sisters.

In every generation the same kind of story would be repeated. The animals with some kind of advantage had a better chance of surviving to reproduce. Thus, over the generations, there would be more and more animals with stronger claws and more and more which could run faster. Slowly, slowly, through new combinations of genes and new mutations, the two varieties could become more and more different until they were so different that they could not breed with one another any more. They would have become too different from each other and so would have become different species.

These variations in plants and animals which accumulate over the generations and gradually lead to different species are called evolutionary changes. It is hard for us to think of things taking millions and millions of years to happen, but only in this way was it possible to produce the great variety of plant and animal life on earth today.

Miacis, shown here, was a prehistoric meat-eating animal that lived in trees and was probably the ancestor of Cynodictis, from which the weasel family apparently came. Cynodictis lived in the period between 36 million and 58 million years ago.

What about the evolution of the Mustelidae? We do not know much about their early ancestors, but the chances are that they were shaped much like the weasels of today and were meat-eaters. Very early in their evolutionary history, closely related forms of these animals began to develop different ways of life. Over a long period of time some kinds became better and better hunters. These evolved into the modern weasels, ferrets, minks, and martens. Other kinds became better and better diggers and began to eat other kinds of food. These developed into badgers and skunks. Members of still a third branch of the family gradually became experts at swimming and catching food in the water. These became the river otters and sea otters. The weasel family's bodies and habits have changed and made them suited to many different ways of life.

There are many kinds of mustelids which will not be discussed at length in this book. Very little is known about most of the South American, African, and Asian mustelids, and there is little chance that you would ever come across them in a zoo. Some of these animals are quite different from the more familiar members of the weasel family.

There are the stink badgers, found in the Malayan islands, which can spray a very offensive musk, as you might guess from their name. The tayra, found in Mexico, Central, and South America, has long, slender legs and a long tail. It can climb and swim well and eats many different kinds of food. The grison, also found in Mexico and down into South America, has a coat of quite long, gray fur, with a black face and chest. This

The grison, a South American mustelid. Like those of the zoril, tayra, and other mustelids from Asia, Africa, and South America, this animal's habits in the wild are not much known. However, it can be observed in captivity, since it is not hard to tame.

animal is easily tamed and apparently makes a good pet. Unlike most members of the weasel family, both tayras and grisons are quite sociable animals and often travel in small groups.

Opening the Wilderness for Fur

The fur of many mustelids is valued for its thick, soft, richly colored beauty. In the eighteenth and nineteenth centuries, one thing that drove forward the explorers of western North America was the search for furs. The pelt of the beaver (not a mustelid but a very large rodent) was the most coveted of all. But many mustelids were also trapped, especially minks, otters, and fishers.

The purpose of many great explorers, such as Lewis and Clark, was mainly to investigate possibilities for the fur trade in the unexplored parts of North America. Great companies, such as the Hudson's Bay Company of Canada, and great fortunes, such as that of the Astor family, were founded on the fur trade.

One of the finest furs is that of the sea otter. The story of how almost every last one of these lively and charming creatures was killed for its fur can teach us something about man and nature—and the need to plan carefully the use of our natural resources for the future.

In 1741, two ships of the great Russian explorer Vitus Bering (after whom the Bering Sea was named) were looking for the west coast of America. They were in the far northern waters near Alaska. The two ships got separated from each other one night. One of them returned to Russia, but the other one was wrecked on a small island. The sailors went ashore and built shelters from the pieces of the broken ship.

They looked around for food, and found a strange animal living in the shallow water near the island. The animals were not afraid of men, so it was very easy for the sailors to hit them over the head and kill them. The sailors enjoyed the meat and they were truly delighted with the beautiful, soft fur which covered their bodies. The fur from the sea otters helped the men keep warm throughout the long, hard winter, although Vitus Bering and many others did not survive.

The sailors built themselves a new boat during the winter and left the island in the spring. On their way home they were

The killing of sea otters—by clubbing and later by shooting—began about 1741 and went on without restraint until it was forbidden by law early in this century. The animals are now increasing.

thrilled to find that the Chinese would pay very high prices for the sea otter pelts which they brought with them from the island. The Russians too were excited by the lovely furs, and many ships headed for the northern seas in search of the animals. They were killed by the thousands, and still more and more ships came to the Pacific coast in search of them. The crew of Captain Cook, who explored much of the Pacific coast, also managed to make a great deal of money selling sea otter pelts to the Chinese.

In this way more and more was learned about the Pacific coast of America, all the way down into California. But in the meanwhile there were fewer and fewer of the otters to be found. The slaughter went on until the early 1900s, when it was feared that these unusual animals would become extinct. Laws were passed which restricted the killing of them. Many people were afraid that the laws had come too late, but fortunately the hardy otters were able to breed and multiply. Now there are several thousand in the northern seas, and there are even some along the California coast.

We were lucky in the case of the sea otter. Hunting and trapping have also reduced the numbers of other mustelids, especially the marten, the fisher, and the river otter. The cutting down of so many of our forests has also lessened the number of martens and fishers, while the pollution of our rivers and streams has greatly reduced the living space of the river otter. In many areas where they used to be common, river otters are no longer seen.

There are people who will say that we would be better off without "varmints" like the weasel or the otter anyway. They declare that the weasel is a bloodthirsty animal which kills innocent creatures for the fun of it, and that the otter is especially fond of eating "our" fish, like trout and bass.

Many farmers hate weasels because once in a while a weasel gets into a henhouse and kills many chickens. But other farmers are happy to have weasels around because they realize that they kill great numbers of mice and other pests. If one does go "bad" and starts wiping out chickens, he can always be shot, but most weasels by far will stick to their natural food and keep down the number of mice.

The fisherman who wishes there were no otters does not realize that most of the fish eaten by the otter are not the big, swift game fish. After all, they are hard to catch. The otter eats mostly the fish that are easiest to catch, such as small mudfish, which are of no interest to the sportsman. As a matter of fact, some of these fish compete for food with the game fish, so in the long run the otters are probably a help to the fishermen.

All the different kinds of plants and animals developed over millions and millions of years. The life of one species affects the life of another, and these relationships evolved as the species did. Most of the problems we find today concerning the scarcity or overabundance of plants or animals are a result of our interfering with the delicate balance which has gradually emerged. This balance includes natural ups and downs of population in various species. But human interference has too often resulted in unnaturally large changes in the size of animal populations.

Some people feel that predators—animals which hunt and kill other animals to eat—are bad simply because they kill. But this is not true. The predators as a group help the prey species because they kill the old, weak, and sick animals, which of course are the easiest to catch. Without predators, the sick animals live longer and make other animals sick. If the weaker animals survive long enough to breed, they will pass on their less desirable traits to their offspring, weakening large parts of the population.

Also, if too many animals live, there is not enough food to go around, and they die the slow, painful death of starvation. Or the prey species can multiply so fast that they become pests to man. Such things have happened in many areas with deer, mice, porcupines, and other creatures. Predators are just as important and necessary in nature as any other type of animal.

2 THE GREAT CHASERS

Weasels, polecats, ferrets, minks, martens, fishers

Many members of the weasel family are completely or almost completely meat-eaters. In order to survive, they must be expert hunters. They have an excellent sense of smell with which to sniff out their prey, and they can run very fast in order to capture it.

The weasels, polecats, and ferrets, which live largely on or under the ground, are long and slim and can follow mice and other rodents right into their burrows. Larger predators, such as coyotes and bobcats, lose out if they cannot catch a mouse before it gets to its burrow, but a weasel can follow it wherever it goes until it is caught. This ability to squeeze through narrow spaces has led to the use of the phrase "to weasel out of it," meaning to get out of doing something you have to do. Weasels can climb trees, too, but fishers and martens are the best tree-climbers of the mustelids.

The size range of the hunting mustelids is very great, all the way from the very small least weasel to the hefty fisher. As a matter of fact, the least weasel is the smallest living member of the order Carnivora. A really big one is nine inches long, including his tail, and weighs only two and one-half ounces. Most weigh under two ounces and are about six inches long. An aver-

The least weasel lives on mice and shrews in the colder months and includes insects in its diet when they are plentiful with the coming of summer.

age male fisher (females are about half the size of males) is three feet long and weighs about 15 pounds. It would take about 120 least weasels to equal the weight of one fisher.

The Long, Lithe Weasels

There are about ten different kinds of weasels, three of which are found in North America. These are the least weasel, the short-tailed, and the long-tailed weasel. The long-tailed weasel is the largest, but even it weighs less than one pound. The variations in weight of long- and short-tailed weasels are very great in different parts of the country. The farther north they are found, the bigger they are, and the greater the size difference between the males and females.

The larger size of the males may enable them to feed on bigger prey than the females, thus reducing the competition for food between the sexes. The larger male can eat big rodents such as ground squirrels. The smaller female can more easily invade small rodent burrows and kill the young. In this way she can more easily feed her own brood. This same principle might explain the size differences between males and females in other mustelids, such as the fisher, as well.

The least weasel is a rich brown color above and pure white on its underside. The stubby tail is brown without a black tip, and the feet are white. The short-tailed weasel is more variable in color, but it is usually brown above with a black tail tip. The underparts are white, sometimes tinged with yellow. The front feet are white and the hind feet light brown.

Long-tailed weasels are the most variable of all, but can be distinguished from the short-tailed species by the longer tail, darker underside, and dark feet. In some areas they have striking facial markings.

Ounce for ounce, no creature can surpass the ferocity of a weasel. A mother will attack even a man if he threatens her young. They are swift and efficient killers and often kill more than they can eat at the moment, storing the rest for later use. This habit of storing food is called "caching," and is common among mustelids.

There is a persistent myth that the weasel is a great destroyer, killing for the sake of killing and sucking the blood from its innocent victims. This image of the weasel can be found almost everywhere, even in the writings of early naturalists. If you call someone a weasel, it is a great insult, for a weasel is supposed to be mean, sneaky, and untrustworthy. No wild creature is by nature evil—each has its place and behaves the way it does simply in order to survive. Let us examine the way of life of the weasel and see where the truth actually lies.

The long-tailed weasel, like the other weasel species, is a very graceful animal.

Weasels tend to be nocturnal (active at night), but they also often hunt in the daytime. Except when raising a family they are solitary creatures. A weasel will live in one burrow until almost all the rodents in an area have been eaten. Then it will leave to find a new home where food is plentiful. Thus, except in a bad year when its food is scarce everywhere, a weasel will leave chickens completely alone and just clear out the rats and mice on a farm before moving on. When one does kill chickens, it is nearly always a large male long-tailed weasel that is the culprit. Although all weasels are well able to kill prey larger than themselves, most of them are just too small to tackle a chicken.

Weasels sometimes do kill large numbers of rodents in one night and eat them. When a person sees the chewed-up remains of many mice lying around on the ground and notes the footprints of a weasel nearby, he naturally thinks the animal has been killing for the fun of it. How could such a small animal eat so many mice at one time? But what the observer fails to realize is that the weasel is a very small, thin, highly active, warm-blooded animal and therefore requires tremendous amounts of food, relative to his size, in order to stay alive. It takes a great deal of energy just to keep such a small, thin body warm.

Weasels in captivity require one-third to one-half their own weight in food a day. Because of its greater activity and the colder air out of doors, a wild weasel would need even more food to survive. The same is true of certain other small mammals and birds. The hummingbird, which is the smallest warm-blooded animal, eats almost constantly while awake. At night its body temperature drops and its metabolism, or process of turning food into energy, slows down greatly; otherwise it would probably starve to death in its sleep.

As mentioned before, a weasel will sometimes enter a hen-house and kill many chickens, many more than it could possibly eat or cache. This is used as evidence of the bloodthirsty nature of the animal. But a henhouse is an artificial, man-made enclosure for chickens. It is not a natural thing that a wild weasel would normally encounter. A caged weasel, if provided with many more mice than it can eat, will also kill them all, even if it is not very hungry. But again, this is an unnatural situation. If we think in terms of the survival of a wild weasel, this kind of behavior makes complete sense.

For example, let's suppose it is early summer and the mother weasel has four hungry, growing young to feed. She runs back and forth along the ground, sniffing intently, until she picks up the scent of a female mouse. She then follows the trail of the mouse as it winds through the grass and enters a burrow. At the end of the trail is the mother mouse with a nest of half-grown young. The weasel quickly grabs the female mouse by the back of her neck and bites down hard, cutting through her spinal cord and killing her. Then she kills each of the young mice the same way, before they can escape. After that she begins to eat. When she is full she carries the rest of the dead mice to her own nest to feed her hungry offspring.

If the mother weasel had killed just one mouse and then started to eat it, the others might have escaped. She then would not have had enough food for herself and her own young. So it is the most natural thing for the weasel to kill all the animals in an enclosed area before eating any. Any uneaten prey can be cached and used later when food may be scarce. In the cool, damp burrow of the weasel, dead mice will probably keep for several days before the meat spoils, and the chances are that it would be eaten before then.

As for the notion of blood-sucking by weasels, there is no scientific support for it. This idea probably arises from the way in which weasels kill. All mustelids use the efficient technique of

To bite its prey at the back of the neck—a habit of mustelids—this short-tailed weasel is approaching from the rear. In the case of rabbits it must be especially careful, for the bulging eyes of rabbits allow them to see to the rear and the front as well as to the sides.

grabbing an animal by the back of the neck and hanging on until the spinal cord is cut through or the animal bleeds to death. Sometimes this takes quite a while, especially when the prey is large. Thus a weasel can be seen, with its teeth buried in the bloody fur of the prey, hanging on as the animal gets weaker and weaker and finally dies. To a human observer, it may look as if the weasel is sucking the blood out of the victim. This impression is made stronger by the fact that the prey may be as large as or larger than the weasel, and the human cannot believe that the weasel could eat it all.

Weasels have proven to be very successful animals in many different kinds of places. They are found in the Arctic and other northern areas, and throughout the United States and Mexico in all but the most extreme desert climates. The long-tailed weasel lives from the northern areas of Canada to as far south as Lake Titicaca in South America. It is truly remarkable that any wild species can live in such varied areas. The only parts of the world where no weasels are found are Antarctica, Australia, most oceanic islands, and the southern halves of Africa and South America. In these last areas, other mustelids somewhat similar to weasels are found.

People often think of weasels as silent, stealthy creatures which never make a sound except for a vicious snarl when cornered. This is far from the truth. Weasels can travel silently while stalking prey, but they also make a variety of sounds which tell other weasels how they feel. For example, the least weasel has four basic sounds it uses. When disturbed, it will give a loud, harsh chirp which means "Don't bother me." The mother may warn her young to leave her alone this way, or may use it to warn an intruder that she will attack if he does not leave. A hiss shows fright when the animal is threatened or retreating.

Weasels can be friendly too, and at such times they make a soft, trilling sound which may last a couple of seconds. When a mother calls her young or when two friendly adult weasels meet, they trill. Finally, if a least weasel is unpleasantly surprised or injured, it will let out a squeal. Other kinds of weasels too use similar sounds to communicate with one another.

Polecats and Ferrets

The polecat and the ferret are very similar in appearance and habits to the weasels. They are larger, however. Polecats are found in Europe, Asia, and North Africa. There are several closely related kinds found in different regions. They can reach a total length of 27 inches and weigh as much as three pounds. They are dark brown or black in color. The facial markings differ with the breed, but often there is a yellow spot on each side of the face between the ear and eye.

The ferret is a variety of the polecat which has been tamed to serve man. It has been domesticated for about two thousand years. In the first century A.D., polecats were used to help eliminate a plague of rabbits in the Balearic Islands. They were used by Genghis Khan in 1221 and by Emperor Frederick II in 1245, probably for rabbit-hunting. The colonial settlers of America used ferrets to control the rodents on their ships. They have been used occasionally on American farms for this purpose, but their main use has been in Europe for hunting rabbits and for killing rats and mice. The ability of the ferret to enter a burrow and force out whatever creature lives in it has led to the phrase "to ferret out," meaning to search out facts that are difficult to uncover.

The black-footed ferret is a very rare and interesting animal which lives in prairie-dog towns on the plains of the United

States and has never been domesticated. It seems that this animal was always rare, but with the efforts of the government and ranchers to eliminate prairie dogs, the black-footed ferret has almost reached the point of extinction. This mink-sized animal has a black mask across its face and a black tip to its tail, as well as black feet. The body is a yellowish tan color, darker above than below. We will investigate the way of life of this creature and its relationship with the prairie dog later.

The Mink

Everyone knows of the mink because of its especially lovely fur. Fortunately for wild minks, man has learned how to raise these animals on ranches. This has reduced the trapping of the wild-living ones considerably, although many of them even today end up as part of a coat. Minks differ from the other animals we have discussed here in that they are as much at home in the water as they are on land. Their fur is thick and warm, so it protects them well from the cold water.

Minks can pursue their prey effortlessly under water. When fishing, a mink will often stand on a rock in the water, watching intently for fish, frogs, or tadpoles. When a tasty item swims by, the mink will dive beneath the water in a flash, surfacing with its catch in its mouth. After setting aside its prey it will resume fishing, gradually accumulating a pile of food. Sometimes a fisherman will do the hard work for the mink. All the animal has to do is to drag the handy string of fish off to his den while the sportsman's attention is elsewhere. The mink is a great hoarder and will cache large numbers of fish, muskrats, and other food in its den for future use.

Minks include eggs in their diet when they can.

The muskrat is one of the favorite foods of the mink. It is a water-dwelling rodent that usually weighs about two pounds. Since this is also the weight of an average mink, quite a battle can result when these two animals meet. In spring and early summer, minks will feast on birds' eggs and young ducks and geese, when they are abundant. Minks can also hunt successfully on land and will eat mice, rabbits, and other small animals. They can climb trees in order to catch a bird or raid a nest. Part of their biological success is due to this ability to make use of whatever food sources there are at a given time.

Although ranch minks have been bred in several different colors, wild minks are shiny dark brown with a white spot on the chin and often one on the chest or the belly as well. Male minks range up to 28 inches in length and three and a half pounds in weight. The females are smaller.

Minks are found in all parts of North America where there are forests and permanent water. They almost always stick close to water in the thick underbrush along streams, small rivers, small lakes, salt marshes, or along the seashore. They hunt in one area until food becomes scarce, then move on to better hunting grounds. Females tend to stay at home in one territory, while males range widely and rarely use the same den twice. There are many dens along a stream which are used by first one, then another male at different times. These are usually made— probably originally by muskrats—under roots of trees along the stream bank. They have more than one entrance, so the mink can escape if necessary.

There is a native species of mink in Europe, but American minks live wild there too, the descendents of ranch minks which escaped or were set free. The European mink is somewhat smaller, and in many areas where American minks have established themselves the European type has been pushed out by its larger cousin.

Martens and Fishers

The marten and the fisher are closely related animals which differ from weasels, ferrets, polecats, and minks in several ways. Their ears are larger, their tails longer and bushier. Both martens and fishers are expert tree climbers. Both will eat berries and nuts as well as meat.

Red squirrels are among the rodents that martens feed on.

There are about seven kinds of martens—sometimes called sables—in the world, and most of them have valuable fur. The Siberian sable has one of the most beautiful furs in the world. For this reason it has been extensively trapped. The American marten, which lives in the forests of the northern United States and Canada, has a pelt which is not quite as valuable as sable.

Martens are especially easy to trap. They do not have the wariness of the mink or the wolverine which helps protect these animals. Because of this, martens at one time were very scarce in North America. But strict limits on trapping have led to their increase.

Martens must have forests to live, and their range has been reduced by our cutting down enormous numbers of trees. On the other hand, since they stay away from houses and barns and do not kill poultry or disturb man in other ways, martens are not hated and killed by people the way weasels are.

Although martens are expert tree-climbers, they spend most of their time on the ground. They are fast enough in the trees to capture red squirrels frequently, but mice make up most of their food. They will also eat beetles, caterpillars, carrion (rotting animal bodies), nuts, and berries. They live alone, except when the female is raising her young.

The adults vary in size. A big marten can be as long as three feet, including its tail. They weigh from one-half to four and a half pounds. As with so many other mustelids, the female is considerably smaller than the male.

The fisher is a real giant. No one seems to know how this animal got its name, for it doesn't catch fish. (However, it will eat dead fish if it finds them.)

When traveling, the fisher often follows streams and lake shores. Like the American marten, the fisher lives in the forests of Canada and the northern United States. Although it can climb quite well, the fisher spends less time in the trees than does the marten. However, it is quick enough above ground to catch the speedy martens and eat them. The main food of the fisher consists of grouse, snowshow hares, mice, and red squirrels. As you will see later, the fisher is a specialist at preying on the porcupine as well.

3 THE STINKER, THE DIGGER, AND THE DEVIL

Skunks, badgers, wolverines

Each of the animals discussed in this chapter has a reputation based on his special way of life. They also have a few things in common: they are more stocky than the hunting mustelids, and each has a distinctive color pattern. All, except for the American badger, are omnivorous; that is, they eat many different kinds of food, including meat, carrion, eggs, fruit, and insects. However, each of these animals has a unique place in the make-up of nature.

The Skunk

The striking black and white coat of the skunk is very familiar to Americans, as is its unforgettable odor. Other mustelids sometimes use their unpleasant musk to help ward off enemies, but in the skunks this technique has reached its highest development.

There are basically three different kinds of skunks. The most common and familiar type is the striped skunk, which is found from southern Canada and throughout the United States to northern Mexico. The spotted skunk lives in parts of southern Canada and the United States, Mexico, and Central America.

37

Few Americans have encountered the hog-nosed skunk, as it is strictly nocturnal and is found only in the southwestern states and down to the tip of South America.

When people think of the skunk, they usually picture a striped skunk. What they think about him is another matter, depending on their personal experiences. Children and city folk usually consider the striped skunk to be a handsome, friendly, somewhat amusing fellow that can make a nice pet if his musk glands are removed. But the hunter or farmer whose dogs have

Striped skunks include beetles and other insects in their very varied diet. The young—generally about four to six are born—grow rapidly.

made the mistake of trying to catch a skunk and then come running back to their masters for some comfort takes a much dimmer view. So does the motorist who is so often made aware of the many skunks killed by cars along highways and country roads.

Both images are correct. He is a handsome fellow and goes his own way as long as he does not feel threatened. But if he decides he cannot escape from real or imagined danger with his slow, lumbering gate, he will turn and face the intruder with his tail held high and his back arched. He will stamp the ground rapidly with his front feet and slowly shuffle backward. If his enemy does not take the hint and leave right away, the skunk will turn around and let him have it with his defensive spray.

Many have commented on the amazing accuracy of the skunk's aim, but what the animal actually does is to spray over a wide area to the rear, so that anything within ten feet behind gets sprayed. The musk has a very strong, unpleasant, and long-lasting smell which is never forgotten once encountered. If it strikes the eyes it can cause a burning sensation, but it does not actually damage them permanently. This defense is very effective, for once an animal or a person has been sprayed by a skunk he will avoid a repeat performance at any cost.

Striped skunks have adapted very well to the presence of man. If anything, they have increased in number with the coming of civilization to America. There are two reasons for this. First, skunks are not afraid of people and often live near houses. They have such confidence in their special defense that sometimes they even make their den right under a house. Also, they thrive in areas where the land is broken up into small woods and fields.

Because of skunks' feeding habits, farmers' fields offer a perfect hunting ground for them. Like many other mustelids, they adapt their diet to the time of year. In the spring they take advantage of the plowing, which destroys the homes of many mice and other small mammals. These displaced creatures are forced to live along the fence rows where the plows cannot reach, and here the skunks can catch them. Nesting birds and their eggs are also eaten at this time. In the late summer and autumn they feast on beetles, grasshoppers, and other insects. Striped skunks have been seen rolling wooly caterpillars in the dirt until the bristly hairs are removed before eating them. Toads are also rolled to squeeze out and remove the irritating chemical in the skin. Along with raccoons, striped skunks sometimes frequent caves and eat bats which have fallen, both at the entrance and inside the cave.

Unlike many mustelids, skunks do not cache food for later use. But since they do not rely mainly on agile rodents for food and have little to fear from enemies, skunks can put on a lot of fat. It doesn't matter if they slow down a bit, especially in the fall when they subsist mainly on a diet of insects. Since their food is very scarce in the wintertime, skunks eat and eat, stuffing themselves and gaining a great deal of weight in the autumn.

During the winter they live in places where they are somewhat protected from the bitter cold, such as in underground dens, under buildings, or under large piles of brush. Often several skunks will be found in the same den. They sleep a lot and may remain in the same den as long as three months without venturing out in the snow. When leaving the den, they most likely will stay within a mile of it, even if they move on to a different one. They find little or nothing to eat during the winter, and when spring comes and the snow melts, a typical skunk weighs half as much as it did when winter began.

In the early spring the skunks leave their winter dens and are more likely to be found living alone than together. Later on, the females give birth to their young, but the males remain solitary.

Striped skunks often measure thirty inches long, including an eight- to ten-inch tail, and can weigh ten pounds in the fall. They move quite slowly—ten miles an hour when running fast —and cannot climb trees.

The spotted skunk is quite a different fellow. He is less than two feet long, including his bushy tail, and weighs under three pounds. He is much more agile and active than the striped skunk and often climbs trees in search of bird nests.

Both types of skunk have very variable color patterns. Basically, the striped skunk has a small white stripe on the forehead, with a white patch on the top of its head that divides into two stripes running along the sides of the back. The tail has very long black and white hairs. Some striped skunks have almost no side stripes, however, while others have stripes so wide that the whole back appears white. All variations in between are found. The spotted skunk has a white patch between the eyes, a black tail with a white tip, and white stripes and spots on its body. The pattern of spots and stripes is so variable that no two spotted skunks are exactly alike.

Since he is more agile than his striped cousin, the spotted skunk can more easily catch small mammals such as rabbits, mice, and rats. These form a large part of his diet, although he also eats insects, eggs, mushrooms, and fruit. The spotted skunk has at least one clever feeding habit of his own. When provided with an egg which is too large for him to bite into, the spotted skunk has been known to kick the egg backwards under his body, giving it a final push with a hind leg. This is done repeatedly until the egg hits something which cracks it. Then the skunk opens up a small hole in the egg and uses his tongue to lap out the contents.

The spotted skunk is more nocturnal in his habits than the striped and is less abundant. He is most likely to be found living on the plains, where he frequents gullies and brushy places. He can be found in just about any place where he can find food, however, including the woods or the beach.

When it comes to defending himself, the spotted skunk has his own way of warning enemies to get out of the way. If the swift raising of his plumed, white-tipped tail does not get the message across, he will stand on his front feet with his menacing rear end up in the air. He may even take a few steps forward on

The spotted skunk, found in the South and Southwest, may do a "handstand" as a warning to a predator. If this doesn't work, it sprays its musk at the intruder.

his forepaws. If all this fails, he will let the intruder have it with a spray of musk which is just as powerful and long-lasting as that of the striped skunk.

The hog-nosed skunk is slightly larger than the striped species. It does not have a white mark on its face, and the fur is quite coarse. It is black below, with either two white stripes or a solid white stripe running down the back. The most distinctive feature of the hog-nosed skunk is its long, hairless, broad nose. This skunk specializes in eating insects, especially those which

The hog-nosed skunk will eat mice or other prey when it cannot get its favorite food, insects.

hide in the ground, such as beetles and insect larvae. It uses its snout to probe insect holes and sniff out the inhabitants. It eats beetles by the hundreds, but it will also consume other food, such as cactus fruit and mice when the opportunity comes along.

Badgers

The fastest-digging hunter in the world is the American badger, and the Old World badger digs tremendously complicated networks of tunnels in which to live. Their digging ability and their similar appearance are just about the only things these two badgers have in common, however.

Both have stocky, somewhat flattened bodies, coarse hair, and short tails. Badger fur is so stiff that it is used to make shaving brushes. Both have grayish upper parts, but the Old World badger has black legs and underparts, while the American badger is light underneath with white patches. The face of the Old World species is striped with black and white, while its American cousin has one white stripe running from its nose to its shoulders and black patches on its face and cheeks.

There are other kinds of badgers too, which are found in Asia—the ferret badget, the hog badger, and the stink badger—but little is known about these animals.

The Old World badger is found in most parts of Europe and also in parts of Asia, including China. It is a big animal, measuring as long as 40 inches and weighing as much as 40 pounds. The home of these badgers is a complex burrow system called a set, and these may be inhabited by several generations. Sets are usually dug in hills with a good cover of concealing plants or trees, especially on southern slopes. One of these homes can extend under an area of many acres and have ten or more entrances.

With its broad, muscular body and efficient digging feet, the badger is a strong fighter and has few enemies. Its largely underground life is an additional protection against attack.

In front of the entrances, large mounds of earth can be found which have built up over the years of digging.

Most of the digging is done in the autumn, when more soil is removed from the set and added to the mound. The large sets are produced gradually over a period of years by the regular addition of new holes and chambers. Dry grass, moss, and leaves are used for bedding. If this gets damp, it is taken out into the sunshine to dry and then reused. As you might expect, other animals take advantage of these fine, large burrows and make their homes in them too. Foxes in particular are common in badger sets, and rabbits, rats, and mice are sometimes found there, as well as many kinds of insects.

Old World badgers are not choosy about food—they eat young rabbits, small rodents, worms, insects, carrion, roots, seeds, and berries. They are playful creatures, especially when young, and the grass near a set entrance may be beaten down by their romping. The young play in the sunlight and gradually shift their activities to evening as they grow up.

While the Old World badger usually inhabits wooded regions, the American species generally lives in dry, open country, although it can be found in the woods as well. It is smaller than the European kind, usually solitary and most often active in the afternoon and at night. It moves around quite a bit—in one study of badger life, the daily activities of a female were followed from summer through winter. In the summer she wandered over an area of 1,880 acres and never used the same den two nights in a row. During the fall this badger moved about much less and stayed within a 130-acre area. She often used the same dens over again. When winter came, she stayed within an area of only five acres and rarely traveled. At this time she used a single den.

All her dens were very simple. Most of them had only one entrance, which the badger plugged up with dirt when she was inside. She apparently did not use any grass or other material to make a nest for herself in any of her homes.

The American badger is better specialized for fast digging than the Old World badger, and for a good reason—it is almost completely carnivorous. Most of its food consists of ground squirrels, mice, and cottontail rabbits which it digs out of the ground. It has to be able to dig fast to catch up with an expert digger such as the ground squirrel. These badgers also eat insects, snakes, birds, and possibly a small amount of plant material. They have been seen catching fish as well.

The Wolverine

Many legends are told in the far north of the strength, fierceness, and cunning of the wolverine. This animal has probably inspired more hatred, fear, awe, and admiration among those who have encountered it than all the other mustelids put together.

Trappers hate the wolverine because it follows their trap lines, eating the animals which have been caught and tearing up their hides so that they are worthless. The animals it cannot eat immediately it takes away and caches for later use. Sometimes it breaks into a trapper's cabin, tearing everything to pieces in its search for food and spraying musk on the food it cannot eat at the time or carry off. This makes the food inedible by any creature but a wolverine. In addition to all this, when the trapper sets out to snare this troublesome beast, he is in for a battle of the wits with one of nature's most cunning creatures. A wary wolverine can often figure out how to get the bait out of a trap without getting caught in it, so the trapper not only fails to catch the pest, he loses his bait too.

Because of the way they are sometimes plagued by a wolverine, some of these men believe it is the spirit of a dead trapper returned to earth to pay for his sins by tormenting other trappers. They say that the dead trapper is freed from those sins when the wolverine is killed, but that it is part of his punish-

An arctic fox, trapped or free, is not too large a kind of prey for wolverines, nor is a deer or an elk. They are fierce, cunning, and the most powerful of the Mustelids.

ment to do everything he can to avoid being caught. Since he lived many years collecting furs, this spirit knows all the tricks of the trade; he is almost impossible to snare.

Some Indians fear the wolverine, and they too think that it is an evil spirit. In some Indian languages it is given a name meaning "a tough thing," and others call him "The Evil One," or the Indian devil. Some think that the wolverine is the lost soul of a once great hunter who now enjoys plaguing other hunters and driving them crazy. Other Indians called him "the invulnerable beast" and made sacrifices to his spirit. They wore his hide in order to take on some of his strength and cleverness.

Another name for the wolverine is "glutton," since some thought he gorged himself on food, probably not realizing that the animal would eat part of a carcass and take away the rest to hide for later use. In the Rocky Mountain states the wolverine is sometimes called the skunk-bear. This name is quite appropriate, for in shape it looks like a small bear, but its long, thick, dark fur has a light band of color which extends from the shoulders along each side of its body, meeting just above the bushy tail. This gives the wolverine a somewhat skunklike appearance. Likewise, its musk smells just as unpleasant as that of the skunk.

Aside from the sea otter, the wolverine is the largest mustelid. A big male can weigh as much as 60 pounds, though about half this is the more usual size. The animal—it is not very common—is found throughout the cold, snowy, northern portions of the world. Its scarcity is really not surprising, since the food supply in these areas is quite limited, and it takes about eighty square miles of land to support one male wolverine. He shares this territory with two or three females, each of which stays in her own area. The wolverine must wander many miles a day to find food, so it needs its tireless strength in order to survive.

Part of the success of these remarkable animals lies in the adaptability of their diet. In the spring they eat the eggs of ground-nesting birds. In the summer they feast on the larvae of wasps, and in the fall, on berries. In all seasons, rodents, fish, frogs, and carrion are eaten. During the winter the wolverine displays great strength and cunning in the way it succeeds in

One of many ways that the wolverine plagues trappers is to gnaw through the ropes of a bundle of food supplies that has been hung on a branch for safety. The bundle usually bursts open when it hits the ground and the wolverine has choice foods with little trouble.

preying on animals many times its own size. It climbs up a tree and crouches on a branch overhanging a game trail. When a young or hunger-weakened deer or moose comes along, hampered by the deep snow, the alert wolverine springs down onto the back of the animal. While hanging on with its powerful claws, it bites the back of the neck of the giant prey in true mustelid fashion and chews until the spinal cord is severed or the animal bleeds to death. Since a medium-sized moose can weigh half a ton, killing an animal about 20 times its own weight is quite a feat for a predator. The successful hunter eats its fill and caches the rest of the carcass for later consumption.

The strength and bravery of the wolverine are truly amazing. It is as strong as a man and can drag a three-hundred pound deer carcass through the snow. It can gnaw through big logs to get at a trapper's food cache or break into his cabin. It will fight any animals which threaten its food supply, and a female will defend her young against all comers, even a man. Wolverines have been seen scaring off bears, wolves, and mountain lions from food.

The trapper may hate this formidable creature for destroying his catch and raiding his cabin, but the wolverine is only feeding himself in the easiest way possible. It contaminates everything in the trapper's cabin or food cache with musk, but this is just the animal's way of marking that food as its own so that no other animal will touch it before it returns to eat it later. We can admire the wolverine for its intelligence, strength, bravery, and tireless energy; without these qualities, it could never survive in the harsh, frozen northland where it lives.

4   THE PLAYFUL OTTERS

Sea otters, river otters

The inquisitive otter is one of the best known and most loved of all wild creatures. Otters are found everywhere except in Antarctica and the extreme Arctic, Australia and New Zealand, the oceanic islands, and very dry desert areas, such as parts of North Africa and the southwestern United States. Otters and water go together; wherever you find one, the other is likely to be nearby. In rivers, lakes, large streams, marshes, and along the coast—in all these places you can find otters. The sea otter is the most aquatic mustelid, for he rarely leaves the water at all. Other kinds of otters often live along the seashore, however.

The other thing which otters have in common, besides a love of water, is a real sense of fun and a need to play, even as adults. Most mammals play as youngsters. Play is very necessary to help them develop their muscles and practice the skills which they will need as adults for hunting, escaping from enemies, and mating. However, few creatures carry this fun-loving spirit into adulthood. The Old World badger is one exception which has already been mentioned, but the real champion of play is the otter.

This is one reason people enjoy otters so much. They can identify with and appreciate the otter's playful spirit and intense curiosity about the world. Otters easily develop an affectionate attachment to people, and man has used this tendency to his advantage for centuries. In ancient China otters were used to catch fish for men. As early as 1480 in Europe, otters were trained to drive fish into nets.

The man who has helped more than any other to popularize the otter is Gavin Maxwell, who wrote of life with his two pet otters in *Ring of Bright Water*. The book was so popular that it was made into a movie.

His otters were of quite different kinds. One was from Iraq and belonged to a species closely related to the common American and European otters. The other was a clawless otter from Africa, a species with front paws which are remarkably similar in their use and appearance to human hands. However different their origins, both were very spirited and affectionate pets. They enjoyed playing with people and would invent games to share. They also liked to amuse themselves, rolling marbles and other small objects endlessly around in their paws or splashing and swimming gracefully in the water.

Many people have kept otters as pets, but an otter is demanding and requires much more human attention than a dog or a cat. It also needs a lot of space, including a place to swim, in order to let out its tremendous energy. Sometimes a pet otter will turn vicious and attack a person without apparent reason. After *Ring of Bright Water*, Gavin Maxwell had more pet otters, and he describes in a later book how two of them seriously injured people. From this you can see that however charming they may be, otters are not good pets for most people.

Otters are quite vocal animals, and different species can make similar sounds. They make a birdlike chirping sound which has many meanings, and they scream when angry. A happy chuckle and a snort of surprise or alarm are also part of their vocal communication.

The River Otter

The North American species of otter is called the Canadian or river otter. Its original range extended from the far north of Canada and Alaska down through all parts of the United States, except desert areas of the Southwest. Now, however, it has vanished in many former parts of its range because of trapping and water pollution.

The river otter weighs between ten and 30 pounds and may grow to be four feet long, with the broad, strong tail making up about one-third of that length. The fur is uniformly short and is usually dark brown above and brownish gray below, although lighter specimens are frequently found. Fun-loving though it may be, the otter is a courageous, strong animal. A 20-pound otter can vanquish a 90-pound dog.

Like other mustelids, the otter makes its home in an underground den; however, this is found along a waterway and has its entrance under water. Some mustelids, such as the American badger and the skunk, may wander quite a bit in the summer but restrict their activities to one small area in the wintertime. Otters do just the opposite. In the summertime they tend to spend most of their time in one area—near a good-sized lake, for instance, or along one particular part of a river. But in the winter they may travel along 50 to 60 miles of stream searching for food. If they live in an area where food is more plentiful, they will travel less.

Although otters have a reputation as happy-go-lucky creatures, life in the winter can be very difficult for them, as it is for other animals. During a very cold spell, an otter may spend all of its time either in its den or hunting for food in the water under the ice. Since water in motion does not get much colder

Mud-sliding is a favorite sport of river otters.

than 32° F. without freezing, the otter is warmer there than it would be out on the surface, where the temperature could be well below zero. Because the den is underground, it too is insulated from the outside temperature. No otter or other water-dwelling mammal comes out of the water onto the land when the air temperature is very cold. Its wet fur could then freeze and no longer protect it from death by cold.

In the dead of winter in the North, otters are too busy hunting to spend much time playing. But in less severe climates and seasons they are experts at having fun. They play hide-and-seek in the snow, and one will conceal a fish from another.

The most well-known and common otter sport is sliding. Sometimes they slide in the snow, but it is hard to know if signs of this on the snow surface are the result of play or merely of travel. When otters go from place to place in the winter, they alternate runs with slides across the snow and ice. This is apparently an easier way for them to travel than just running or walking.

In any case, the summer mud-sliding of otters is pure fun. A group will pick a muddy bank on a stream or lake and go swooping down it, landing with a splash in the water. Then they dash out of the water and rush up to the top of the bank to wait their turn to slide again. The more sliding is done, the smoother and more slippery the slide becomes, and the more fun the otters have. They can keep up this activity for an hour or more at a time. Groups of otters also play splashing and chasing games in the water, and when alone they will fondle and retrieve small objects such as smooth stones, apparently just for fun.

Though fishermen blame the otter for eating many game fish, this accusation is unjust. Biologists checked on this over a period of six years in Wisconsin, Michigan, and Minnesota. They found that fish, especially nongame fish, were the main food of otters in these areas, and crayfish, frogs, and aquatic insects were important sources of food. Game fish were not often eaten. Otters are almost completely carnivorous, but they probably eat some berries and maybe pond plants as well. They also have been known to eat waterfowl, especially young ducks in the springtime.

The Sea Otter

This mustelid wears what is usually considered the most desirable fur coat in the world. In the first chapter we saw how they almost became extinct as a result. From their original range along the entire Pacific coast from California to Alaska, the otters were reduced to a few animals sheltered in rocky coves along the Canadian, Alaskan, and Siberian shores, and to a small, isolated colony at Big Sur, a rugged part of the California coast. Although their number is constantly increasing now, they will probably never reinhabit all of their former range due to pollution of areas heavily used by man.

This otter weighs as much as 80 pounds and sometimes measures up to four and a half feet in length, including a foot-long tail. It is the biggest of the mustelids. Its fur is black to dark brown, except for a grayish head, throat, and chest. Its body is well adapted for swimming, for its tail is flattened and its hind feet are webbed and are used like flippers for swimming.

Nowadays sea otters spend most of their time in the water, leaving it to give birth and perhaps occasionally for other purposes. Courtship and mating take place in the water. The first naturalist to study the sea otter, however, said that they spent a great deal of time on shore. His name was Georg Steller, and he was a member of the expedition which spent that bitter winter on Bering Island. He had a lot of time to study marine animals during his stay, and was the first to describe Steller's sea cow (now extinct), the sea lion, and the fur seal, as well as the sea otter.

Some of what Steller writes must be true, as Bering's sailors killed the sea otters with clubs as they lay on the beaches. Other early travelers and fur hunters also comment that the otters

The sea otter is thoroughly at home in the water and spends most of its time there.

hauled themselves up on the beaches in large bands just like fur seals. Either because they have learned to fear man over the years or because all the shore-loving otters were killed off and left no progeny, they are rarely found on shore in California. In the North, however, they often rest or sleep on land.

Sea otters are just as playful as their freshwater cousins. They splash about in the water and toss balls of kelp around. They

The sea otter sometimes uses a very clever method of opening up a sea urchin. Those that live in more southerly waters eat mostly urchins and clams; those of northern waters use fish as their principal food.

enjoy one another's company, and the adults are very affectionate with their young. The mother's fearless protection of her pup often led to her death when she was hunted. Alone, an adult could escape from the hunter's boat, but a mother otter would never abandon her young, and thus she would die at the hands of the hunters.

Although they live in the water, sea otters do not go far out from shore. They prefer to live in the kelp beds near land, within a half mile of the coast. They dive for their food, but not in deep water. Sea urchins, which are relatives of sea stars and look like hard, spiny balls, are a favorite food. Fish, shrimps, and clams are also eaten.

The otters eat floating on their backs and sometimes place rocks on their chests on which they bang clams or sea urchins until the shell cracks. (Using a rock this way is sometimes considered to be animal use of a tool.) Then they suck out the soft insides and toss the shell away. Other foods are snails, crabs, fish eggs, and occasionally fish. Sea otters need to eat one-fifth to one-fourth of their body weight a day, probably because they need a lot of energy to keep up a proper temperature in the cold water. Their only protection from the cold is a layer of air trapped in their dense fur. They lack the insulating layer of fat under the skin that other marine mammals, such as seals and whales, have. They must be very careful to keep their fur clean; if it gets matted with food grease and debris. much of the air is expelled and the otter can get chilled.

5 PREYING AND COOPERATING

All mustelids are to some degree hunters and are well equipped for self-defense, but at times they do become the prey of other hunters. Weasels, minks, and the young of larger mustelids often become prey of the great horned owl in America and the eagle owl in Europe. These are the largest owls and often have a wingspread of five and a half feet. They swoop down silently from the sky with amazing speed and capture their prey with their sharp, curved beaks and large, strong claws. The great horned owl will prey on skunks too if it is desperate.

Golden eagles, which have a wingspread of over six feet, prey on polecats, badgers, weasels, and martens. Red foxes, coyotes, bobcats, and cougars are all enemies of mustelids in the United States. Only the wolverine—at least as an adult—seems to be almost free of natural enemies. Even a mountain lion would be foolish to tackle a full-grown wolverine.

Mustelids also include one another in their diets. Wolverines will eat otters, and otters sometimes eat minks. One of the foods of fishers, when they can get it, is marten. Badgers, if they are hungry enough, will attack skunks.

*Weasels and minks especially are in danger from the great horned owl;
their alertness and speed are not always sufficient to avoid capture.*

Fishers and Their Porcupine Prey

Although most hunting mustelids will eat just about anything
they can catch, some have favorite foods. The fisher, for example, is an expert porcupine-killer. In one study of the fisher's

eating habits, porcupine hair and quills were found in 30 per cent of the stomachs examined. You can see that the porcupine is an important source of food to the fisher.

The porcupine has a tremendously effective coat of armor in the quills which cover its upper body and tail. Most predators will avoid this animal unless they are very hungry, and if they do eat it they often die from quills piercing the walls of their stomachs and intestines. The fisher, however, knows how to flip a porcupine over on its back and attack its soft underside before its prey can right itself. Somehow, too, the fisher's intestines are rarely damaged by the quills if they are swallowed.

The fisher knows how to get the better of a porcupine, whose quills make it a very difficult kind of prey.

In some states, such as Wisconsin, fishers were just about eliminated by hunting and trapping. Porcupines became more and more common and were destroying valuable timber by gnawing all the way around the tree trunks, killing the trees. To remedy this, fishers were trapped in areas where they were still relatively common and were released where there were too many porcupines. Now the fisher has been re-established in many of these forests and the porcupine population has been reduced to a more reasonable level. Keep in mind, however, that the increase in porcupine population might have been due in part to a natural cycle of abundance.

Minks and Muskrats

As we have seen, one of the most common prey of the mink is the muskrat. Muskrats usually weigh about two pounds but sometimes grow to about twice that weight; they can look very much like giant rats. They live in swamps and along the edges of waterways, in mounds of plant material or in dens dug in the banks. Their homes have tunnels leading to the outside, which open under water.

Muskrats are very fertile animals which produce several litters of young every year. The social arrangements of a muskrat colony are quite complicated, and the weakest animals are driven away from the best muskrat areas and thus are forced to live in less desirable places. It is these "exiled" muskrats which become prey to the mink roaming the shores of the swamps.

During the wintertime one can sometimes see where minks have dug into muskrat houses, dragged out the inhabitants and eaten them. People assume that the minks killed the muskrats, but it turns out that in these cases the muskrats were already dead from disease, and the minks just dug out the carcasses.

Muskrats that have been forced into a solitary life are the ones most likely to be victims of hungry minks.

After all, a mink and a muskrat are about the same size, and the muskrat is an able fighter. It is very difficult for a mink to kill just one large, healthy muskrat, much less a whole houseful. So we can see that, although the mink eats muskrats often, it has little or no effect on the population level of this prey species. The weaker muskrats which are forced out of the colony and become prey of the mink would not reproduce anyway, and the muskrats dug out by minks in the winter are already dead.

The Black-Footed Ferret versus the Prairie Dog

The relationship between the black-footed ferret and the prairie dog is a fascinating subject which has only recently been studied. Prairie dogs are rodents which live in large colonies called "dog towns." It is probably "now or never" for scientists interested in the black-footed ferret, for there are very few of these rare animals left.

Little is known of their habits, for they spend most of their lives underground in prairie dog burrows. Only once or twice have they been seen to kill a prairie dog above ground. Apparently almost all of their hunting is done beneath the surface. For this reason, when a ferret is around, the "dogs" stay outside as much as possible. This is in contrast to their behavior when other predators, such as coyotes or bobcats, appear. Then they stay in their burrows, where these large predators cannot reach them. A mother ferret has often been seen entering a burrow, coming up with the dead bodies of one or more prairie dogs, and taking them to the tunnel in which she has put her young. Ferrets always eat their prey underground.

Prairie dogs try to protect themselves by filling up the entrances to the burrows in which ferrets live, but the ferrets can easily dig themselves out. Once in a while the "dogs" will fight with a ferret above ground until it is forced to return to its burrow, but generally these rodents are unable to protect their town from a resident ferret family. The number of prairie dogs in a town which contains a mother ferret and her young can be greatly reduced in population by the end of the summer. At that time the ferrets leave and each goes its own way, searching for a new town to live in.

As the poisoning campaigns wipe out more and more towns, there will be fewer and fewer suitable places for the black-footed ferret to live, and the species will almost certainly be-

The black-footed ferret is only rarely seen above ground and does most of its hunting in prairie dog burrows.

come extinct. These animals do occasionally eat other food, such
as mice, and they may also eat birds, ground squirrels, eggs, and
insects. They have been found living in haystacks or under
barns, but this was usually in the fall, at the time when they are
looking for new homes. Whether it is possible for these ferrets to
survive for long periods of time away from their usual food and
habitat is doubtful.

The Badger and the Coyote

Sometimes different kinds of animals help one another find
food. The mustelids provide two interesting examples of this

*The badger is a good digger but a slow runner; the coyote is just the
reverse. So cooperation works out well.*

kind of interaction between species. There is quite a bit of evidence that the badger and the coyote sometimes hunt together. Old Navajo Indian stories tell of the badger and coyote travelling and hunting together and calling each other "cousin." Many observers in recent years have seen a badger traveling with one or more coyotes.

The coyote can run fast, but it cannot dig out prey that have run into deep burrows. The badger is slow, but it can dig out just about anything if it wants to. Badgers have been seen following coyotes which chased prey into burrows, and coyotes have been seen waiting at one burrow exit while a badger dug at a different one. People have also seen coyotes catch prairie dogs which ran out of burrows being dug out by badgers.

Since coyotes will on occasion eat badgers, it is interesting to wonder how the badger knows that it is sometimes safe with coyotes. Of course these two hunters are not consciously helping each other; they are just taking advantage of one another's hunting talents.

The Honey Badger and the Honey Guide

One of the strangest and most fascinating relationships between two species is that of a small, brownish gray bird of Africa called the honey guide and a mustelid called the honey badger, or ratel, an animal about three feet long.

As you might guess from their names, these animals look for bees' nests, and they work together at this. When the honey guide discovers a nest, it flies off in search of its helper, the ratel. When it finds him, it swoops near and chatters loudly before flying off in the direction of the bees' home. The honey badger follows the bird until they reach the nest, which is usually located in an old, hollow tree trunk.

The entrance is very small—about as big around as a pencil—so the bird would not be able to get to the honey by itself. But the badger has very strong, curved claws with which it climbs the tree and tears open the nest. While the badger works, the honey guide sits on a nearby branch and chatters. The ratel's tough skin protects it from bee stings while it gorges. After it climbs down, the honey guide takes its turn—but it is more interested in eating the beeswax than the honey. It is one of the very few animals that can digest wax.

It is said that the ratel takes a piece of the comb from the nest and stores it in a nearby tree stump for later use. This is very possible, considering the fact that most mustelids do cache food. There is a popular story in Africa that in the rainy season the rainwater mixes with the honey in the hollow of the stump and that the honey ferments into honey beer. When the ratel returns to eat his cache, he gets drunk and runs madly about, tearing up the ground all around the stump. This is the kind of story that is probably best classified as "not proven so far."

If the honey guide cannot find a ratel to help it out, it will fly up to humans or to other animals and try to lead them to the honey. Africans sometimes follow the bird and open up the nest after putting the bees to sleep with smoke from a bit of burning grass. They always leave a piece of the comb stuck on a twig for the honey guide, for they believe that if they do not leave it this gift, the bird will not guide them to any more bees' nests.

The ratel, or honey badger, uncovers the honey after the honey guide leads him to it.

6   WAYS AND MEANS OF SURVIVAL

Each kind of plant and animal is suited to living in a particular sort of place. Fishers and martens are found in the forests, never on the treeless plains. Badgers are found on the plains, never in the deep forests of the north. Otters are found in and near water. Wolverines live in the northland, and are never found in the southern states, while the hog-nosed skunk is found in the hot, dry southwestern part of the United States and never in the cooler, damper north.

Some kinds of animals can live in more varied environments than others. The long-tailed weasel has a tremendous range from north to south, and is successful in warm climates and cold; and the river otter originally was found just about anywhere in the United States and Canada near abundant water. Other animals are not at all adaptable. An extreme example of this is the black-footed ferret, which seems to survive only in the very limited environment of the prairie dog town.

The kind of place in which an animal lives is called its habitat. For example, the habitat of the marten is the dense pine forests of the north, whereas the habitat of the wolverine is the far north, whether it is forested or north of the tree line—the boundary beyond which trees cannot grow. The habitat of a species tells where it lives but not how it lives. For example one species may be very active in the winter and another will sleep away the cold months in the same habitat. Many different kinds of plants and animals share the same habitat.

The description of how the animal lives—what it eats, what eats it, whether it is active by day or by night, and so on—is called its niche. The niche is often compared to a person's occupation, but this is not really a good comparison, because the niche includes so much more. It is not enough to say that the weasel's niche is as a hunter. You must be more specific and say what it hunts and at what time of day, what its enemies are, and many other things about it. To describe completely the niche of an animal is to know all about its way of life and how it affects the other plants and animals and the soil, air, and other nonliving parts of its environment. We do not know enough about any living thing to describe its niche completely, but the idea of the niche is useful in comparing the way of life of different animals.

It is said that no two species which live in the same area can occupy the same niche, and this is probably true. Even if the way of life of two species seems very much the same, close study would probably reveal some important differences. Evolution has been going on now for so long that the most successful species have replaced less successful ones. (Evolution is, of course, still going on, but generally at a rate too slow for one person to see in his lifetime. It is possible to see evolution in some living things, such as bacteria, which have a very short generation time, but for practical purposes we can talk as if the evolution of the animals we speak about was finished. We should always keep in mind, however, the fact that evolution is a continuing process which never ends.)

Furs and Tails

When we study different animals, we can see that they are adapted to their different habitats, and how they are adapted. For example, the fur of mustelids which live in similar habitats is similar in some ways, whereas mustelids living in different habitats have very different fur. The hair of the hog-nosed skunk and the honey badger is coarse and thinner than that of other mustelids; these animals live in hot, dry climates. The most luxuriant mustelid furs are those of the sea otter, river otter, and mink; these are water-living animals which need thick, close coats to protect them from the cold water. The pelts of mustelids which live in cold, northern climates are more valued than those from the south because they are thicker.

The fur of the wolverine, which lives farther north than any other mustelid, has a unique property which is useful to man as well as to the wolverine itself. When it is very cold and frost forms on the fur, it does not stick and can be easily brushed off. For this reason, wolverine fur is in demand for trimming parka hoods. With other kinds, moisture in the breath of the person wearing the parka condenses on the trim as ice. When the person goes indoors, the ice melts and makes the fur wet and soggy.

The tails of mustelids are also suited to their differing habitats. Otters have strong, flattened, or thick tails which they use as rudders in swimming. Tree-climbing mustelids such as the marten and fisher have very bushy tails which they use as rudders and parachutes in the trees. The long-tailed weasel is also a tree-climber and has a longer tail than the purely ground-dwelling short-tailed weasel. Badgers, which spend so much of their lives underground and have no special use for a tail, except as a brace when sitting up on their haunches, have short tails.

Feet, Teeth, and Claws

By looking at the feet of an animal, you can get a pretty good idea of its habitat. The marten has strong, curved claws on all four feet which provide a firm grip while it climbs. Also, the soles of its feet are hairy, and this may keep it from slipping on smooth branches. The feet of the wolverine are broad and furred on the soles; they serve as natural snowshoes.

Otters' feet are webbed between the toes, which is an aid in swimming; the sea otter's hind feet are long, broad, and flipper-like. The hind feet of river otters from the North have small, rough bumps on them which help prevent slipping when the animals walk on ice. Southern river otters from Mexico and Central America, which never encounter cold winters, lack these bumps on their feet. Otters can close their nostrils and their ears when they swim under water. This is another way in which they are especially suited to their habitat.

Evolution has also accommodated animals to fit the different niches they have come to occupy. The most important aspect of the niche is probably what food a particular kind of animal eats and how it goes about getting it. One thing all mustelids, except perhaps the striped and hog-nosed skunks, have in common is their great activity. Everyone who writes about these creatures comments on their constant alertness and boundless energy. It is very important to a hunter to have tremendous reserves of energy, as it must be able to outlast its prey. The great hunting success of the weasel is largely due to its constant motion. It hunts by trotting back and forth along the ground, zig-zagging its way across the fields until it comes across the fresh scent of a mouse or other prey. Then it follows the trail until it comes across the animal which made it. The wolverine can cover tre-

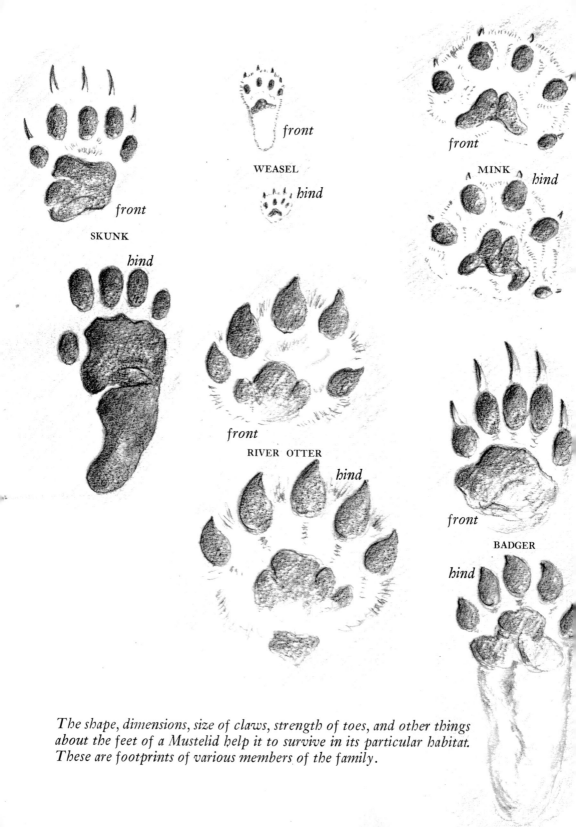

front

WEASEL

hind

front

MINK

hind

front

hind

SKUNK

front

RIVER OTTER

hind

front

BADGER

hind

The shape, dimensions, size of claws, strength of toes, and other things about the feet of a Mustelid help it to survive in its particular habitat. These are footprints of various members of the family.

mendous distances in one day and really has to in order to find enough food in the barren North.

Most mustelids have a sharp sense of smell that helps them find their prey; and the otter has very good close-up vision and sensitive, agile front paws that expertly catch the small crayfish and other water life upon which it feeds.

Teeth and claws are important tools to a predator. The needle-sharp claws of the weasel aid it in holding onto its prey. The skunk and badger have long, thick, slightly curved claws on their front feet that make them fine for digging. The American badger, which relies so much on fast digging to catch its prey and escape from enemies, has larger, more powerful front feet than the Old World badger.

The teeth of hunting mustelids have evolved into excellent tools for a meat diet. The front teeth (incisors) are the biting teeth and can tear flesh. The canine teeth (eyeteeth) are long and sharply pointed; they easily pierce skin and muscle, and hold onto the prey. (The wolverine uses its canine teeth not only to hunt but also to pierce eggs for sucking.) The premolars and/or molars, depending on the species, are flattened vertically and bladelike. The top teeth act with the bottom ones like a pair of shears to cut the flesh.

Weasels, which eat only meat, lack molars in the back of the jaw; but the otter has these teeth, which are broad enough for crushing crayfish shells and fish bones. The molars of the sea otter are especially large and flat, fine for crushing the shells of sea urchins, clams, and other food.

Protecting itself from enemies is absolutely necessary if a creature is to survive. One way to get protection is to hide, and this is certainly one function of the burrows used by so many different kinds of animals. Another way to hide is to have a color that blends with the surroundings. Most mustelids have coats of

The short-tailed weasel is called an ermine when its coat turns almost entirely to white in the winter, though sometimes the word is applied to the white-coated form of the least and the more northerly long-tailed weasels also. The change of its coat with the season is an adaptation that gives it considerable protection. At the bottom it is seen in its summer coloring.

some shade of brown. The black and white coat of the skunk is an exception, but it is to his advantage to advertise who he is because of his powerful musk. In the northern parts of their range, weasels turn white in the winter, whereas those in the south do not. The white coats not only protect them from predators but also make it harder for their prey to see them. Unfortunately for weasels, however, in the past man has valued this white winter coat so much that it was considered fit only for royalty. This fur, especially when from one of the species of weasel with a black tail tip, is called ermine. The demand for it has decreased in recent years as royal pomp and ceremony has decreased, although it is also used to some extent for less regal apparel.

If they are actually attacked, all mustelids put up a good fight. Their sharp and powerful teeth and claws and their rapid, agile movements certainly help them in life-and-death struggles. Some are also protected by another adaptation: the honey badger, American badger, wolverine, and perhaps others have very tough skin which is hard to pierce. Not only that, but the skin of these mustelids and also of the otter is attached to the body inside at only a few points, so that even if one of them is bitten in the back of the neck, it can turn right around—"in its skin," so to speak—and bite back.

A Protective Chemical

The unpleasant musk which is characteristic of the weasel family is produced within a pair of scent glands, one on either side of the anus, or outer opening of the intestine. When the animal wants to spray its musk, the glands are pushed out and squeezed by muscles, releasing the spray. Some other carnivores (such as the mongoose and its relatives, the civets) have similar

The striped skunk gives a warning in several ways before it finally squirts its musk, as it is doing here.

glands. Musk probably serves to protect somewhat even those animals which have not made a specialty of smelling bad.

All mustelids will release their musk if frightened or attacked, and the resulting smell is never pleasant. The skunk is probably the only mustelid whose musk has been developed to the point of being an almost foolproof protection, however. Musk is present even in new-born skunks, and by the time they are just two weeks old it can be expelled. By twenty-five days of age, before they can stand up, they can raise their tails in warning and can release a few drops of musk.

This fluid is useful in other ways as well. Mustelids mark the borders of their territories with their scent glands; if another member of the species comes along, it can tell by the strength and quality of the lingering odor how long ago the last animal was there and whether it was a male or a female. Otters make extensive use of scenting stations in any place that is greatly used—at mud slides or in front of their dens, for instance. Often an otter will make a little mound of sand on which to scent. Trappers have learned of this habit and use the scenting stations to tell if otters are nearby. Badgers, wolverines, and some weasels also mark their caches with their musk. Not only does this mark the claim as their own, it also makes the food unpaltable to other animals.

7   CONTINUING THE SPECIES

If animals cannot produce more of their own kind to replace themselves, their species will eventually die out. Thus the species which exist today have evolved effective ways of producing and raising young. Sometimes we cannot figure out why a particular aspect of a species' reproduction is successful, but time has proven its usefulness.

Most mustelids live alone as adults, so there have to be ways for the males and females to get together to mate. Different species mate at various times of the year. Striped skunks and minks mate in the winter. At this time the animals spend a lot of time in dens, and the females stay in a much more limited area than the males. The chances are that in their wandering the males will come across dens which are occupied by females. Then mating can take place, and the young will be born in early spring.

For good reasons, young animals of most kinds are born in the spring. This is a time of renewed growth for all kinds of living things, so food is abundant. Also, plenty of time is available for the young to grow big and strong enough, as well as wise enough, to live through their first winter. The least weasel breeds in the early spring. It does not take long for its young to develop, be born, and grow up. As a matter of fact, these weasels often produce two litters a year. The larger a mustelid is, the longer it takes for the developing young (called an embryo, in its earliest stages; later a fetus) to reach birth weight. It also takes large animals longer to grow to independence after birth, so larger mustelids living a solitary life even in the winter have a problem. Winter mating is impractical, but mating in the spring would result in the young being born too late to grow up sufficiently before winter. Since the period of time it takes for the embryo to develop is from one to perhaps three months in these animals, mating in the summer or fall would result in the young being born in the fall or winter. Other kinds of animals, such as seals and some deer, face the same difficulty.

A Stop-Go Embryo

Nature has solved the problem, so to speak, by lengthening the period of pregnancy for these animals. In this way they can mate in the summer or fall and still give birth in the spring. Slowing the actual development of the embryo would require many complicated changes, but stopping it for a certain period is much simpler. This, in fact, is what has happened in many species of animals, including mustelids such as the American marten, fisher, wolverine, river otter, badger, short-tailed weasel, and long-tailed weasel.

The method used to suspend the development of the embryo is called delayed implantation. After a mammal egg cell is fertilized, it divides several times and forms a mass of cells with a cavity in the center. This very early embryo is called a blastocyst. For these blastocysts to continue growing (two or more develop at a time in various mother mustelids) they must receive nourishment from an outside source. Unlike bird, amphibian, and reptile eggs, mammals' eggs (except in the two rare egg-laying mammals) contain little yolk for nourishing the embryos. Therefore the mother's body must provide what the embryos need for growth.

Each blastocyst becomes embedded in the lining of the uterus—the organ in which the unborn animal develops—and blood vessels from the mother bring nutrients to it. This process of the blastocyst embedding itself in the lining of the uterus is called implantation. In delayed implantation, the blastocysts remain in the uterus without implanting for weeks or months. Then, when the days begin to get longer and spring will come soon, the little balls of cells implant and begin developing into young weasels, skunks, or other mustelids.

Thus, many mustelids have a very long gestation period (the time from fertilization of the egg until birth). It ranges from eight months in the American badger to as long as twelve months in the river otter. Mysteries remain still, however, as to the reasons why some animals have delayed implantation and others do not. The Old World weasel often lives in climates as severe as those in the northern United States, but it never shows delayed implantation. Another puzzling case is that of the spotted skunk. In eastern forms, mating occurs in the spring, and the young are born from the middle of June through July. In the West, however, the animals mate in the early fall, and delayed implantation occurs. Birth takes place in western forms about the middle of May. To further complicate matters, spotted skunks in the southwest may breed in July, and in the southeast, females may have two litters in one year. There the climate is mild enough for two litters to develop successfully in one season, but it is hard to see why the western animals should have delayed implantation and the eastern animals lack it.

The sea otter breeds all year around. This may seem strange, since this animal often lives so far north, where the winter is long and the climate cold. But since the sea otter spends almost all its time in the water, the passing seasons do not affect it as much as they do a land animal. Also, the waters along the Alaskan coast are warmer than might be expected because of the Japan current, a mass of warm water which moves along the coast of Japan and across the Pacific to Alaska.

The sea otter produces one, or rarely two, offspring at a time, and the mother takes especially good care of her young. The young are born in the water and need a lot of attention or they would not survive.

Other mustelids produce varying numbers of young, depending on the species and the area they inhabit. For example, the striped skunk usually has four to six offspring, but a litter of

The young of this striped skunk, like the young of almost all Mustelids, are helpless when born, and their eyes remain closed for a time.

sixteen has been recorded. Generally speaking, the smaller mustelids produce bigger litters than the larger ones. Thus, wolverines and river otters usually produce two to four young, although otters may have as many as five. Weasels, on the other hand, produce from four to nine young in a litter.

All the young, except the sea otter pup, are born blind and helpless. They have little or no fur on their bodies and cannot stand up. They are completely dependent on their mother and at first drink only her milk. Young weasels grow and mature very fast, and female long-tailed weasels mate at three or four months of age. They become mothers the following spring, before they are a year old. Other weasels and American badgers also mate before they are a year old. Wolverines and fishers mate after their first birthday, while river otters and martens do not mate until they are two years old.

Diligent Mothers

However long it takes for the young to grow up, all mustelid mothers are well known for their fierce and fearless attachment to their young. In some species the males also help out with the family, but in others they do not. Male weasels have been seen bringing food to a den where young are being reared. The chances are that in such a case it is not the father of these young that is helping. Since short-tailed and long-tailed weasel females mated the previous year, they have been pregnant for nine to eleven months. Considering the solitary life led by the animals between the mating season and the birth of the young, it seems highly unlikely that the true father weasel would still be nearby.

The mother skunk takes care of the young all by herself. She has a very strong maternal urge, and striped skunk mothers have been known to adopt lost or motherless baby skunks, both in captivity and in the wild. When the young are about two months old, they accompany the mother on hunting trips. The mother leads and they follow her in a line. By fall, the family breaks up and the young skunks are on their own.

Otters have very close family ties, but the mother takes care of the young by herself when they are small. The babies' eyes open at five weeks of age, and they begin to play with one another. By the time the otters are four months old, the mother lets them out of the den and teaches them to swim. At first they are afraid of the water, but they learn fast. When the young are five months old, they are ready to learn to fish and slide, and both parents teach them. Most mustelid families break up in the late summer or fall and the animals make their own way during the winter. Otter families, however, sometimes stay together in the winter, and young wolverines take more than a year to be completely independent of their mother.

Learning to Hunt

The skills involved in hunting are partly inherited and partly learned. Young mustelids spend a great deal of time playing, and most of their play is aggressive. Play-fighting is important to the young animals for two reasons. First, it helps strengthen and develop their muscles as they grow. Second, it helps them perfect their inherited skills and learn other skills.

For example, as young polecats grow, they show complete patterns of aggressive behavior without having to watch other polecats. This indicates that these patterns are inherited rather than learned. However, if polecats are taken away from their mother and littermates when a few weeks old, they are very slow at learning to bite prey on the neck when they are old enough to hunt. A polecat raised with his littermates learns the neck bite faster. Young polecats must also learn to recognize their prey. At first they will chase any animal which is running away from them. If a young polecat sees a rat sitting still, he will walk up and sniff at it. If the rat runs toward him, he will run away. Only after the polecat has killed a rat does he recognize it as prey. Then he will attack rats whatever their behavior is.

Some aspects of mating behavior must also be learned. Mink ranchers have found that if they take male minks away from their families before they are nine weeks old, the males often do not mate successfully with females at first. A scientist who studied this problem concluded that the play of mink kits (the young) between five and eight or nine weeks is very important in developing correct mating behavior. The same is true for polecats. In both species, isolated males bite the female anywhere instead of on the neck as they should. When the male bites the female on the neck, she holds still so mating can take place, but if he bites her elsewhere, she moves around. The males which have been isolated must learn from the behavior of the females that the neck is the correct place to bite, whereas those raised with their littermates have learned the correct behavior through their play.

The study of the importance of play and of teaching by parents in animals is a fairly new and challenging field. Animals such as insects do not play and are not taught by their parents. Their behavior is "programmed" into their nervous systems, which produce it automatically, somewhat like a computer. Mammals, on the other hand, do play as babies and are dependent on their mother or on both parents for food, protection, and education. Some of their behavior is "programmed" and some is learned. Such animals are more flexible in their ability to adapt to all kinds of situations; they can learn to meet crises and solve problems. This adaptability is extremely important for the survival of such animals in an environment that is constantly and sometimes abruptly changing.

SUGGESTED READING

Jane Annixter and Paul Annixter, *Sea Otter* (Holiday House, 1972)

Robert Buell and Charlotte Skladal, *Sea Otters and the China Trade* (McKay, 1968)

Carroll Colby, *Fur and Fury* (Duell, 1963)

Phil Drabble, *Badgers at My Window* (Taplinger, 1970)

Michael Frome, *The Varmints: Our Unwanted Wildlife* (Coward-McCann, 1964)

Lilo Hess, *The Misunderstood Skunk* (Scribner, 1969)

Peter Krott, *Demon of the North* (Knopf, 1959)

Joseph Lippincott, *Striped Coat, the Skunk* (Lippincott, 1954)

Gavin Maxwell, *Ring of Bright Water* (Young Reader's Edition, Dutton, 1961)

Ed Park, *The World of the Otter* (Lippincott, 1971)

Charles Ripper, *The Weasel Family* (Morrow, 1959)

Alice Seed, compiler, *Sea Otter: In Eastern North Pacific Waters* (Pacific Search, 1972)

Henry Williamson, *Tarka the Otter* (Random, 1960)

Dorothy Wisbeski, *The True Story of Okee the Otter* (paperback, Archway, 1968; also hardbound, Farrar, Straus and Giroux, 1967)

INDEX